Published by PJ15 Publishing
info@pj15.com

Preface

First, I'd need to thank the Lord our God for the inspiration and knowledge that enabled me to create this little booklet as well as for the technology that gives us the power to share these thoughts of wise Christians and Bible verses on a scale greater than ever before.

We are able to take this heritage of wisdom with us in our pockets anywhere we go and tap in to it on the moments that we - or others - need it the most.
I like to read one of these quotes in the morning, as food for thought, so to speak. That way I have something that keeps my mind from wandering and it makes a great conversation starter too.

If you like the contents of this book, please share it with our fellow Christians and non-Christians alike. By doing so, you help spreading the Word.
I pray that these Christian quotes will give you strength, wisdom and happiness. And that hereby a little more love may shine throughout the world.

Nicholas Appleyard

†

God, the Eternal God, is Love. Covet therefore that everlasting gift, that one thing which it is certain is going to stand, that one coinage which will be current in the universe when all other coinages of all the nations of the world shall be useless and unhonored.

- Henry Drummond

I cannot imagine how the clockwork of the universe can exist without a clockmaker.

- Voltaire

Though the light shines on things unclean, yet it is not thereby defiled.

- St. Augustine of Hippo

A test of a Christian's character is what he does after he comes to the blockade in the road and what his attitude is after everything has left him except Jesus.

- Lester Roloff

†

Now, God be praised, that to believing souls gives light in darkness, comfort in despair.

- William Shakespeare

And he said, It is not the voice of them that shout for mastery, neither is it the voice of them that cry for being overcome: but the noise of them that sing do I hear.

- Exodus 32:18

True friendship is a plant of slow growth.

- George Washington

When the time comes for you to die, you need not be afraid, because death cannot separate you from God's love.

- Charles Haddon Spurgeon

†

Christians are like the several flowers in a garden
that have each of them the dew of Heaven, which,
being shaken with the wind, they let fall at each
other's roots, whereby they are jointly nourished, and
become nourishers of each other.

- John Bunyan

For a hundred that can bear adversity there is hardly
one that can bear prosperity.

- Thomas Carlyle

Tell the heavens and earth to celebrate and sing!
Command every mountain to join in song.

- Isaiah 49:13

Get all you can, save all you can and give all you can.

- John Wesley

†

I remember my mother's prayers -- and they have always followed me. They have clung to me all my life.

- Abraham Lincoln

You can see God from anywhere if your mind is set to love and obey Him.

- Aiden Wilson Tozer .

God has set the type of marriage everywhere throughout the creation.--Every creature seeks its perfection in another.--The very heavens and earth picture it to us.

- Martin Luther

Many a man curses the rain that falls upon his head, and knows not that it brings abundance to drive away the hunger.

- Saint Basil

†

In whatever direction you turn, you will see God coming to meet you; nothing is void of him, he himself fills all his work.

- Seneca The Younger

A dog barks when his master is attacked. I would be a coward if I saw that God's truth is attacked and yet would remain silent.

- John Calvin

Who falls for love of God shall rise a star.

- Ben Jonson

The men whom I have seen succeed best in life have always been cheerful and hopeful men, who went about their business with a smile on their faces, and took the changes and chances of this mortal life like men, facing rough and smooth alike as it came.

- Charles Kingsley

†

Forget yourself and live for others, for It is more blessed to give than to receive.

- Albert Benjamin Simpson

We seek peace, knowing that peace is the climate of freedom.

- Dwight David Eisenhower

The purpose of life is to live it, to taste experience to the utmost, to reach out eagerly and without fear for newer and richer experience.

- Eleanor Roosevelt

A little lifting of the heart suffices; a little remembrance of God, one act of inward worship are prayers which, however short, are nevertheless acceptable to God.

- Brother Lawrence

†

Nothing is so strong as gentleness. Nothing is so gentle as real strength.

- Frances de Sales

Habits of thought are not less tyrannical than other habits, and a time comes when return is impossible, even to the strongest will.

- Alexander Vinet

To worship God in truth is to recognize Him for being who He is, and to recognize ourselves for what we are.

- Brother Lawrence

You can give without loving, but you cannot love without giving.

- Amy Carmichael

†

A good example is like a bell that calls many to church.

- Unknown

No one is useless in this world who lightens the burden of it for anyone else.

- Charles Dickens

Let us have faith that right makes might; and, let us to the end dare to do our duty.

- Abraham Lincoln

I could not say I believe. I know! I have had the experience of being gripped by something that is stronger than myself, something that people call God.

- Carl Jung

†

It always strikes me, and it is very peculiar, that when we see the image of indescribable and unutterable desolation - of loneliness, of poverty and misery, the end of all things, or their extreme - then rises in our mind the thought of God.

- Vincent van Gogh

All sunshine makes the desert.

- Leaves of Gold

Afflictions are but the shadows of God's wings.

- George Macdonald

Prayer is a shield to the soul, a sacrifice to God, and a scourge for Satan.

- John Bunyan

†

Let your hearts revive and live.

- Psalm 69:32

Personal liberty is not personal license.

- Billy Sunday

I thank God every time I remember you. In all my prayers for all of you, I always pray with joy

- Philippians 1:3-4

The anvil is not afraid of the hammer.

- Charles Spurgeon

The Psalms are like a mirror, in which one can see oneself and the movements of one's own heart.

- Athanasius

†

Yes, I will bless the LORD and not forget the glorious things He does for me. He forgives all my sins. He heals me.

- Psalm 103:2-3

When large numbers of people share their joy in common, the happiness of each is greater because each adds fuel to the other's flame.

- St. Augustine of Hippo

The law works fear and wrath; grace works hope and mercy.

- Martin Luther

Trust in the LORD with all thine heart; and lean not unto thine own understanding. In all thy ways acknowledge him, and he shall direct thy paths.

- Proverbs 3:5-6

†

And when Jesus had cried with a loud voice, he said, Father, into thy hands I commend my spirit: and having said thus, he gave up the ghost.

- Luke 23:46.

Your word is a lamp to my feet and a light to my path.

- Psalm 119:105

The voice of humility is God's music, and the silence of humility is God's rhetoric.

- Francis Quarles

A truly rich man is one whose children run into his arms when his hands are empty.

- Unknown

†

He who created us without our help will not save us without our consent.

- St. Augustine of Hippo

Forgiving and being forgiven are two names for the same thing. The important thing is that a discord has been resolved.

- Clive Staples Lewis

Write injuries in sand, kindnesses in marble.

- Unknown

If I can put one touch of rosy sunset into the life of any man or woman, I shall feel that I have worked with God.

- George Macdonald

†

Be ever engaged, so that whenever the devil calls he may find you occupied.

- St. Jerome

A man that doth not increase his stock diminisheth it; if you do not improve your stock of grace, your stock will decay. The angels on Jacob's ladder were either ascending or descending; if you do not ascend in religion, you descend.

- Thomas Watson

Trees have their seasons at certain times of the year when they bring forth fruit; but a Christian is for all seasons.

- Ralph Brownrig

†

Is life not full of opportunities for learning love?
Every man and woman every day has a thousand of
them. The world is not a playground; it is a
schoolroom. Life is not a holiday, but an education.
And the one eternal lesson for us all is how better we
can love.

- Henry Drummond

Good duties must not be pressed and beaten out of
us, as the waters came out of the rock when Moses
smote it with his rod; but must freely drop from us,
as myrrh from the tree, or honey from the comb.

- Thomas Watson

Marriage was ordained for a remedy and to increase
the world and for the man to help the woman and
the woman the man, with all love and kindness.

- William Tyndale

†

Hath any wounded thee with injuries? Meet them with patience. Hasty words rankle the wound; soft language dresses it.

- Francis Quarles

Let things true be preferred to things false, things eternal to things momentary, things useful to things agreeable.

- Lucius Caelius Lactantius

Never, never be afraid to do what's right, especially if the well-being of a person or animal is at stake. Society's punishments are small compared to the wounds we inflict on our soul when we look the other way.

- Martin Luther King, Jr

Ambition, the desire to overtop our fellows, to have more than other people have, to be more than other people are, has left a bloodstained trail across history.

- Harry Emerson Fosdick

†

Faith is to believe what you do not see; the reward of this faith is to see what you believe.

- St. Augustine of Hippo

God cannot be comprehended by us, except as far as he accommodates himself to our standard.

- John Calvin

To err is human, to forgive, divine.

- Alexander Pope

Wise leaders should have known that the human heart cannot exist in a vacuum. If Christians are forbidden to enjoy the wine of the Spirit they will turn to the wine of the flesh....Christ died for our hearts and the Holy Spirit wants to come and satisfy them.

- Aiden Wilson Tozer

†

Those who die in Jesus live a larger, fuller, nobler life, by the very cessation of care, change, strife, and struggle.

- Alexander Maclaren

There is no emptiness of soul ever for those whose life is devoted to God.

- William Lawson

To the man who pleases Him, God gives wisdom, knowledge and happiness.

- Ecclesiastes 2:26

We are urgent about the body; He is about the soul. We call for present comforts; He considers our everlasting rest. And therefore when He sends not the very things we ask, He hears us by sending greater than we can ask or think.

- Richard Cecil

†

Love is patient, love is kind. It does not envy, it does not boast, it is not proud.

- 1 Corinthians 13:4

Be patient with everyone, but above all with yourself.

- Francis de Sales

I have found in the Bible words for my inmost thoughts, songs for my joy, utterance for my hidden griefs, and pleadings for my shame and feebleness.

- Samuel Taylor Coleridge

To one who has faith, no explanation is necessary. To one without faith, no explanation is possible.

- Thomas Aquinas

✝

Gratitude is the fairest blossom which springs from the soul.

- Henry Ward Beecher

Compassion costs. It is easy enough to argue, criticize and condemn, but redemption is costly, and comfort draws from the deep. Brains can argue, but It takes heart to comfort.

- Unknown

When love and skill work together expect a masterpiece.

- John Ruskin

Let it not be imagined that the life of a good Christian must be a life of melancholy and gloominess; for he only resigns some pleasures to enjoy others infinitely better.

- Blaise Pascal

†

Involuntary ignorance is not charged against you as a fault; but your fault is this---you neglect to inquire into the things you are ignorant of.

- St. Augustine of Hippo

Be assured, if you walk with Him and look to Him, and expect help from Him, He will never fail you.

- George Mueller

What matters most is a good and ready will to obey God.

- Johannes Tauler

Do all the good you can by all the means you can in all the places you can at all the times you can to all the people you can as long as ever you can.

- John Wesley

†

I will place no value on anything I have or may possess except in relation to the kingdom of Christ.

- David Livingstone

Christ beside me, Christ before me, Christ behind me, Christ within me, Christ beneath me, Christ above me.

- Saint Patrick

Death to a good man is but passing through a dark entry, out of one little dusky room of his Father's house into another that is fair and large, lightsome and glorious, and divinely entertaining.

- Adam Clarke

Few things are impossible to diligence and skill. Great works are performed, not by strength, but perseverance.

- Samuel Johnson

†

Above all, love each other deeply, because love covers over a multitude of sins.

- 1 Peter 4:8

The secret of His presence is a more secure refuge than a thousand Gibraltars. I do not mean that no trials come. They may come in abundance, but they cannot penetrate into the sanctuary of the soul, and we may dwell in perfect peace even in the midst of life's fiercest storms.

- Hannah Whitall Smith

For he that will love life, and see good days, let him refrain his tongue from evil, and his lips that they speak no guile: Let him eschew evil, and do good; let him seek peace, and ensue it.

- 1 Peter 10-11

Never be afraid of giving up your best, and God will give you His better.

- James Hinton

†

Lord, when we are wrong, make us willing to change. And when we are right, make us easy to live with.

- Peter Marshall

Children will follow the example, instead of following the advice.

- Lord Palmerston

Will is to grace as the horse is to the rider.

- St. Augustine of Hippo

To have failed is to have striven, to have striven is to have grown.

- Maltbie Davenport Babcock

Be not proud of race, face, place, or grace.

- Samuel Rutherford

†

To cultivate the sense of the beautiful, is one of the most effectual ways of cultivating an appreciation of the Divine goodness.

- Christian Nestell Bovee

It is a great consolation for me to remember that the Lord, to whom I had drawn near in humble and child-like faith, has suffered and died for me, and that He will look on me in love and compassion.

- Wolfgang Amadeus Mozart

Many persons have a wrong idea of what constitutes true happiness. It is not attained through self-gratification but through fidelity to a worthy purpose.

- Helen Keller

Suffering overcomes the mind's inertia, develops the thinking powers, opens up a new world, and drives the soul to action.

- Anthony Harrison Evans

†

A blessed thing it is for any man or woman to have a friend; one human soul whom we can trust utterly; who knows the best and the worst of us, and who loves us in spite of all our faults; who will speak the honest truth to us, while the world flatters us to our face, and laughs at us behind our back.

- Charles Kingsley

Pride is to character, like the attic to the house - the highest part, and generally the most empty.

- Sydney Howard Gay

Just when the caterpillar thought the world was over, it became a butterfly...

- Proverb

The place of charity, like that of God, is everywhere.

- Francis Quarles

†

Prayer is reaching out after the unseen; fasting is letting go of all that is seen and temporal. Fasting helps express, deepen, confirm the resolution that we are ready to sacrifice anything, even ourselves to attain what we seek for the kingdom of God.

- Andrew Murray

One great power of sin is that it blinds men so that they do not recognize its true character.

- Andrew Murray

Doubt springs from the mind. Faith is the daughter of the soul.

- Unknown

Fear thou not; for I am with thee: be not dismayed; for I am thy God: I will strengthen thee; yea, I will help thee; yea, I will uphold thee with the right hand of my righteousness.

- Isaiah 41:10

†

The whole being of any Christian is faith and love. Faith brings the man to God, love brings him to men.

- Martin Luther

It is riches of the mind only that make a man rich and happy.

- Thomas Fuller

Such is the way with sinners. Everything excites their suspicion; they quake at every shadow; they start at every noise; they look upon every man as an enemy.

- John Chrysostom

Peace cannot be achieved through violence, it can only be attained through understanding.

- Ralph Waldo Emerson

†

All things must come to the soul from its roots, from where it is planted.

- Saint Teresa of Avila

If you can't feed a hundred people, then feed just one.

- Mother Teresa

A Bible that's falling apart usually belongs to someone who isn't.

- Charles Spurgeon

Any faith in Him, however small, is better than any belief about Him, however great.

- George Macdonald

†

Whatever a person may be like, we must still love them because we love God.

- John Calvin

Happy is the man that findeth wisdom, and the man that getteth understanding. For the merchandise of it is better than the merchandise of silver, and the gain thereof than fine gold.

- Proverbs 3:13-14

A tree is known by its fruit; a man by his deeds. A good deed is never lost; he who sows courtesy reaps friendship, and he who plants kindness gathers love.

- Saint Basil

Blessed is the man that endureth temptation: for when he is tried, he shall receive the crown of life, which the Lord hath promised to them that love him.

- James 1:12

†

Heaven must be in me before I can be in heaven.

- Charles Stanford

Love is a fruit in season at all times, and within the reach of every hand.

- Mother Teresa

The greatest thing a man can do for his Heavenly Father is to be kind to some of His other children.

- Henry Drummond

Think not that you shall turn to God when you will, if you will not when you may.

- Gervase Babington

†

When blessed with wealth, let them withdraw from the competition of vanity and be modest, retiring from ostentation, and not be the slaves of fashion.

- William Wilberforce

Good character is property. It is the noblest of all possessions.

- Samuel Smiles

Be at peace with your own soul, then heaven and earth will be at peace with you.

- Saint Jerome

Cold words freeze people, and hot words scorch them, and bitter words make them bitter, and wrathful words make them wrathful. Kind words also produce their own image on men's souls; and a beautiful image it is. They smooth, and quiet, and comfort the hearer.

- Blaise Pascal

†

We should live our lives as though Christ was coming this afternoon.

- Jimmy Carter

Joy, which was the small publicity of the Pagan, is the gigantic secret of the Christian.

- Gilbert Keith Chesterton

Peace of conscience is nothing but the echo of pardoning mercy.

- William Gurnall

Commit to the LORD whatever you do, and your plans will succeed.

- Proverbs 16:3

†

What brings joy to the heart is not so much the friend's gift as the friend's love.

- Saint Alfred

Of two evils choose neither.

- Charles Haddon Spurgeon

The Lord is my light and my salvation; whom shall I fear? The Lord is the stronghold of my life; of whom shall I be afraid?

- Psalm 27:1

Dishonest people conceal their faults from themselves as well as others, honest people know and confess them.

- Christian Nestell Bovee

†

What if you woke up today with only the things you thanked God for yesterday?

- Unknown

There is no more terrible sight than ignorance in action.

- Johann Wolfgang Goethe

He, who cannot forgive a trespass of malice to his enemy, has never yet tasted the most sublime enjoyment of love.

- Johann Kaspar Lavatar

The body of our prayer is the sum of our duty; and as we must ask of God whatsoever we need, so we must watch and labor for all that we ask.

- Jeremy Taylor

†

Some people think God does not like to be troubled with our constant coming and asking. The way to trouble God is not to come at all.

- Dwight Lyman Moody

The desire of love is to give. The desire of lust is to take.

- Unknown

When men sought to make Him a king He fled; now that they seek to put Him to death He goes out to meet them.

- Rudolph Stier

Preach the Gospel, if necessary, use words!

- Saint Francis

†

Let us not ask of the Lord deceitful riches, nor the good things of this world, nor transitory honors; but let us ask for light.

- Gregory Nazianzen

Success is not the key to happiness. Happiness is the key to success. If you love what you are doing, you will be successful.

- Albert Schweitzer

A hot-tempered man stirs up dissension, but a patient man calms a quarrel.

- Proverbs 15:18

A dreadful thing is the love of money! It disables both eyes and ears, and makes men worse to deal with than a wild beast, allowing a man to consider neither conscience nor friendship nor fellowship nor salvation.

- John Chrysostom

†

If your heart takes more pleasure in reading novels, or watching TV, or going to the movies, or talking to friends, rather than just sitting alone with God and embracing Him, sharing His cares and His burdens, weeping and rejoicing with Him, then how are you going to handle forever and ever in His presence...? You'd be bored to tears in heaven, if you're not ecstatic about God now!

- Keith Green

This desire for heart purity is a creation of the Holy Spirit at work in the heart.

- Duncan Campbell

Faith leads us beyond ourselves. It leads us directly to God.

- Pope John Paul II

Knowing the Bible is one thing. Knowing the author another.

- Unknown

†

There is no surprise more magical than the surprise of being loved. It is the finger of God on a man's shoulder.

- Charles Morgan

I don't know what your destiny will be, but one thing I know: the only ones among you who will be really happy are those who will have sought and found how to serve.

- Albert Schweitzer

It is true that we may desire much more. But let us use what we have, and God will give us more.

- Adoniram Judson

God destines us for an end beyond the grasp of reason.

- Thomas Aquinas

†

The idea that everything would happen exactly as it does regardless of whether we pray or not is a specter that haunts the minds of many who sincerely profess belief in God. It makes prayer psychologically impossible, replacing it with dead ritual at best.

- David Brainerd

God sees hearts as we see faces.

- George Herbert

The whole of creation, with all of its laws, is a revelation of God.

- Dean William Ralph Inge

Passion is the evil in adultery. If a man has no opportunity of living with another man's wife, but if it is obvious for some reason that he would like to do so, and would do so if he could, he is no less guilty than if he was caught in the act.

- St. Augustine of Hippo

†

Best of all is it to preserve everything in a pure, still heart, and let there be for every pulse a thanksgiving, and for every breath a song.

- Konrad von Gesner

Humility is the guardian of virtue.

- St. Bernard

Every tomorrow has two handles. We can take hold of it with the handle of anxiety or the handle of faith.

- Henry Ward Beecher

You may depend upon it that he is a good man whose intimate friends are all good, and whose enemies are decidedly bad.

- Johann Kaspar Lavater

†

It has always seemed to me a major tragedy that so many people go through life haunted by the fear of death--only to find when it comes that it's as natural as life itself. For very few are afraid to die when they get to the very end. In all my experience only one seemed to feel any terror--a woman who had done her sister a wrong which it was too late to right. Something strange and beautiful happens to men and women when they come to the end of the road. All fear, all horror disappears. I have often watched a look of happy wonder dawn in their eyes when they realized this was true. It is all part of the goodness of nature and, I believe, of the illimitable goodness of God.

- A Veteran Nurse, Leaves of Gold

What an absurd thing it is to pass over all the valuable parts of a man, and fix our attention on his infirmities.

- Joseph Addison

†

Night and day I pondered until I saw the connection between the justice of God and the statement that 'the just shall live by his faith.' Then I grasped that the justice of God is that righteousness by which through grace and sheer mercy God justifies us through faith. Thereupon I felt myself to be reborn and to have gone through open doors into paradise.

- Martin Luther

I press on toward the goal to win the prize for which God has called me heavenward in Christ Jesus.

- Philippians 3:14

The seeds of kindness that you plant today, will one day bloom in the hearts of all that you touch.

- Unknown

The test of Christian character should be that a man is a joy-bearing agent to the world.

- Henry Ward Beecher

†

No man in the world should be so happy as a man of God. It is one continual source of gladness. He can look up and say, "God is my Father, Christ is my Saviour, and the Church is my mother.

- Dwight Lyman Moody

Do not look back on happiness, or dream of it in the future. You are only sure of today; do not let yourself be cheated out of it.

- Henry Ward Beecher

Humility enforces where neither virtue nor strength can prevail, nor reason.

- Francis Quarles

There is a wealth of unexpressed love in the world. It is one of the chief causes of sorrow evoked by death: what might have been said or might have been done that never can be said or done.

- Arthur Hopkins

†

God will either give us what we ask, or what He knows to be better for us.

- St. Bernard

God loves each of us as if there were only one of us.

- St. Augustine of Hippo

The Lord will grant you abundant prosperity - in the fruit of your womb, the young of your livestock and the crops of your ground - in the land he swore to your forefathers to give you. The Lord will open the heavens, the storehouse of his bounty, to send rain on your land in season and to bless all the work of your hands. You will lend to many nations but will borrow from none.

- Deuteronomy 28:11-12

The cistern contains. The fountain overflows.

- William Blake

†

He whose head is in heaven need not fear to put his feet into the grave.

- Matthew Henry

I want the love that cannot help but love; Loving, like God, for very sake of love.

- Albert Benjamin Simpson

We should so work as if we were to be saved by our works; and so rely on Jesus Christ, as if we did no works.

- Francis Asbury

A man may lose the good things of this life against his will; but if he loses the eternal blessings, he does so with his own consent.

- St. Augustine of Hippo

†

The grass withers, the flower fades, but the word of our God stands forever.

- Isaiah 40:8

God speaks in the silence of the hearth. Listening is the beginning of prayer.

- Mother Teresa

Family education and order are some of the chief means of grace; if these are duly maintained, all the means of grace are likely to prosper and become effectual.

- Jonathan Edwards

Do you wish to be great? Then begin by being. Do you desire to construct a vast and lofty fabric? Think first about the foundations of humility. The higher your structure is to be, the deeper must be its foundation.

- St. Augustine of Hippo

†

God brings men into deep waters not to drown them, but to cleanse them.

- John Hill Aughey

God, the best maker of all marriages, combine your hearts into one.

- William Shakespeare

False friends are like our shadow, keeping close to us when we walk in the sunshine, but leaving us the instant we cross into the shade.

- Christian Nestell Bovee

To be in Christ is the source of the Christian's life; to be like Christ is the sum of His excellence; to be with Christ is the fullness of His joy.

- Charles Hodge

†

Lying to ourselves is more deeply ingrained than lying to others.

- Fyodor Dostoevsky

Hell is paved with good intentions.

- Martin Luther

Hypocrisy desires to seem good rather than to be so; honesty desires to be good rather than seem so.

- Arthur Warwick

If pride turned some of the angels into demons, then humility can doubtless make angels out of demons.

- John Climacus

Grace grows best in winter.

- Samuel Rutherford

†

Lord, who art always the same, give that I know myself, give that I know Thee.

- St. Augustine of Hippo

Be faithful in small things because it is in them that your strength lies.

- Mother Teresa

If there is anything that keeps the mind open to angel visits, and repels the ministry to evil, it is pure human love.

- Nathaniel Parker Willis

What I spent I lost; what I possessed is left to others; what I gave away remains with me.

- Unknown

†

Art, like morality, consists in drawing the line somewhere.

- Gilbert Keith Chesterton

You never hear Jesus say in Pilate's judgement hall one word that would let you imagine that He was sorry that He had undertaken so costly a sacrifice for us. When His hands are pierced, when He is parched with fever, His tongue dried up like a shard of pottery, when His whole body is dissolved into the dust of death, you never hear a groan or a shriek that looks like Jesus is going back on His commitment.

- Charles Haddon Spurgeon

Let us never put confidence in man, or in any sanctity of position, office, or dress. If apostleship did not make Judas a saint, neither will position, office, nor dress make thee a saint.

- Johann Ferus

✝

That my heart may sing to you and not be silent. O Lord my God, I will give you thanks for ever.

- Psalm 30:12

Our deeds are seeds of fate, sown here on earth, but bringing forth their harvest in eternity.

- George Dana Boardman

The safest road to hell is the gradual one... the gentle slope, soft underfoot, without sudden turnings, without milestones, without signposts.

- Clive Staples Lewis

I look to a day when people will not be judged by the color of their skin, but by the content of their character.

- Martin Luther King, Jr

†

To win true peace, a man needs to feel himself directed, pardoned and sustained by a supreme power, to feel himself in the right road, at the point where God would have him be - in order with God and the universe. This faith gives strength and calm.

- Henri Frederic Amiel

The greatest pleasure I have known is to do a good action by stealth, and to have it found out by accident.

- Charles Lamb

Be slow in choosing a friend, slower in changing.

- Benjamin Franklin

Reputation is what men and women think of us; character is what God and the angels know of us.

- Thomas Paine

†

For I know the plans I have for you, declares the Lord. Plans to prosper you and not to harm you, plans to give you hope and a future.

- Jeremiah 29:11

A stumble may prevent a fall.

- Proverb

Let there be kindness in your face, in your eyes, in your smile, in the warmth of your greeting...Don't only give your care, but give your heart as well.

- Mother Teresa

Faith, mighty faith, the promise sees, And looks to God alone; laughs at impossibilities, and cries it shall be done.

- Charles Wesley

†

Enjoy the blessings of this day, if God sends them; and the evils of it bear patiently and sweetly: for this day only is ours, we are dead to yesterday, and we are not yet born to the morrow.

- Jeremy Taylor

Our words are the commentaries on our wills.

- Antony Farindon

Faith is taking the first step even when you don't see the whole staircase.

- Martin Luther King, Jr

Sorrow is our John the Baptist, clad in grim garments, with rough arms, a son of the wilderness, baptizing us with bitter tears, preaching repentance; and behind him comes the gracious, affectionate, healing Lord, speaking peace and joy to the soul.

- Frederic Dan Huntington

†

He that cannot forgive others, breaks the bridge over which he himself must pass if he would reach heaven: for every one has need to be forgiven.

- Thomas Fuller

The gracious, eternal God permits the spirit to green and bloom and to bring forth the most marvellous fruit, surpassing anything a tongue can express and a heart conceive.

- Johannes Tauler

Happiness is like manna; it is to be gathered in grains, and enjoyed every day. It will not keep; it cannot be accumulated; nor have we got to go out of ourselves or into remote places to gather it, since it is rained down from Heaven, at our very doors.

- Tryon Edwards

†

The monstrosity of sexual intercourse outside marriage is that those who indulge in it are trying to isolate one kind of union (the sexual) from all the other kinds of union which were intended to go along with it and make up the total union.

- Clive Staples Lewis

As in the candle I know there is both light and heat, but put out the candle, and they are both gone.

- John Selden

Nothing good ever comes of violence.

- Martin Luther

Blessed is he who considers the poor; The LORD will deliver him in time of trouble. The LORD will preserve him and keep him alive, And he will be blessed on the earth.

- Psalms 41:1-2

†

I believe in Christianity as I believe that the sun has risen: not only because I see it, but because by it I see everything else.

- Clive Staples Lewis

All labor that uplifts humanity has dignity and importance and should be undertaken with painstaking excellence.

- Martin Luther King, Jr

Since much wealth too often proves a snare and an incumbrance in the Christian's race, let him lighten the weight by dispersing abroad and giving to the poor; whereby he will both soften the pilgrimage of his fellow travellers, and speed his own way the faster.

- Augustus Toplady

Conscience is the perfect interpreter of life.

- Karl Barth

✝

Hope is like a road in the country; there was never a road, but when many people walk on it, the road comes into existence.

- Lin Yutang

The mind of him that worketh ill is not always corrupt; but the mind of him that defendeth evil is ever corrupt.

- Lancelot Andrewes

We cannot help conforming ourselves to what we love.

- Francis de Sales

In order to know God, we must often think of Him; and when we come to love Him, we shall then also think of Him often, for our heart will be with our treasure.

- Brother Lawrence

✝

Every tomorrow has two handles. We can take hold of it with the handle of anxiety or the handle of faith.

- Henry Ward Beecher

Isn't it funny how day by day nothing changes, but when you look back everything is different.

- Clive Staples Lewis

Teach us to give and not to count the cost.

- Saint Ignatius

God is not what you imagine or what you think you understand. If you understand, you have failed.

- St. Augustine of Hippo

There is within every soul a thirst for happiness and meaning.

- Thomas Aquinas

†

Affliction comes to us, not to make us sad but sober; not to make us sorry but wise.

- Henry Ward Beecher

The torture of a bad conscience is the hell of a living soul.

- John Calvin

There is no fear in love; but perfect love casteth out fear.

- John 4:18

The chains of love are stronger than the chains of fear.

- William Gurnall

When life gets to hard to stand... Kneel.

- Gordon Bitner Hinckley

†

We sometimes fear to bring our troubles to God, because they must seem so small to Him who sitteth on the circle of the earth. But if they are large enough to vex and endanger our welfare, they are large enough to touch His heart of love.

- Reuben Archer Torrey

Forgiveness does not mean excusing.

- Clive Staples Lewis

There is only one basis for really enjoying life, and that is, to walk in the way in which God leads you. Then you are prepared to find delight in all sorts of wayward incidents. When a man is drifting through life, seeking nothing outside of self-gratification, the world must become increasingly a barren and forbidding wilderness. But it is wonderful how many delights fall to the lot of him who is led by God. For such a one the clasp of a friend's hand, a cool drink in the heat of noon, a merry salutation from a passing traveler, a glimpse of beauty by the road, a quiet resting place at night, are all full of unspeakable pleasure.

†

- Leaves of Gold

A Christian is a perfectly free lord of all, subject to none. A Christian is a perfectly dutiful servant of all, subject of all, subject to all.

- Martin Luther

Help me to work and pray, help me to live each day, that all I do may say, thy Kingdom come.

- Albert Benjamin Simpson

A man may be theologically knowing and spiritually ignorant.

- Stephen Charnock

The little troubles and worries of life may be as stumbling blocks in our way, or we may make them stepping-stones to a nobler character and to Heaven. Troubles are often the tools by which God fashions us for better things.

- Henry Ward Beecher

†

There were ten lepers healed, and only one turned back to give thanks, but it is to be noticed that our Lord did not recall the gift from the other nine because of their lack of gratitude. When we begin to lessen our acts of kindness and helpfulness because we think those who recieve do not properly appreciate what is done for them, it is time to question our own motives.

- Leaves of Gold

My dear Jesus, my Savior, is so deeply written in my heart, that I feel confident, that if my heart were to be cut open and chopped to pieces, the name of Jesus would be found written on every piece.

- Saint Ignatius

I picked up a man from the street, and he was eaten up alive from worms. Nobody could stand him, and he was smelling so badly. I went to him to clean him, and he asked, 'Why do you do this?' I said, 'Because I love you.

- Mother Teresa

†

He is rich or poor according to what he is, not according to what he has.

- Henry Ward Beecher

And I say to you, Ask, and it shall be given you; seek, and ye shall find; knock, and it shall be opened to you. For every one that asketh receiveth; and he that seeketh findeth; and to him that knocketh it shall be opened.

- Luke 11:9-10

True godliness does not turn men out of the world, but enables them to live better in it and excites their endeavors to mend it.

- William Penn

But without faith it is impossible to please him: for he that cometh to God must believe that he is, and that he is a rewarder of them that diligently seek him.

- Hebrews 11:6

✝

Death is the golden key that opens the palace of eternity.

- John Milton

The God who gave us life, gave us liberty at the same time.

- Thomas Jefferson

Your life is short, your duties many, your assistance great, and your reward sure; therefore faint not, hold on and hold up, in ways of well-doing, and heaven shall make amends for all.

- Thomas Brooks

Love takes up where knowledge leaves off.

- Saint Thomas Aquinas

†

O Holy Spirit, descend plentifully into my heart. Enlighten the dark corners of this neglected dwelling and scatter there Thy cheerful beams.

- St. Augustine of Hippo

Eternity to the godly is a day that has no sunset; eternity to the wicked is a night that has no sunrise.

- Thomas Watson

Walk boldly and wisely....There is a hand above that will help you on.

- Philip James Bailey

Christ beats His drum, but He does not press men; Christ is served with volunteers.

- John Donne

✝

Without friends no one would choose to live, though he had all other goods.

- St. Augustine of Hippo

This book [the Bible] will keep you from sin or sin will keep you from this book.

- Dwight Lyman Moody

When I want to speak let me think first. Is it true? Is it kind? Is it necessary? If not, let it be left unsaid.

- Maltbie Davenport Babcock

The truth shall make you free.

- John 8:32

People nowadays take time far more seriously than eternity.

- Thomas Raymond Kelly

†

Young men, be not deceived. Think not you can, at will, serve lusts and pleasures in your beginning, and then go and serve God with ease at your latter end. Think not you can live with Esau, and then die with Jacob...It is an awful mockery to suppose you can give the flower of your strength to the world and the devil, and then put off the King of Kings with the scraps and leavings of your hearts.

- John Charles Ryle

It is no great thing to be humble when you are brought low; but to be humble when you are praised is a great and rare attainment.

- Bernard of Clairvaux

Kind words can be short and easy to speak, but their echoes are truly endless.

- Mother Teresa

†

Tears are often the telescope through which men see far into heaven.

- Henry Ward Beecher

Sin is the mother of all sorrow, and no sort of sin appears to give a man so much misery and pain as the sins of his youth. The foolish acts he did - the time he wasted - the mistakes he made - the bad company he kept - the harm he did himself, both body and soul... all these are things that often embitter the conscience of an old man, throw a gloom on the evening of his days, and fill the later hours of his life with self-reproach and shame.

- John Charles Ryle

Faith does not make things easy, it makes them possible.

- Luke 1:37

✝

Faith fills a man with love for the beauty of its truth, with faith in the truth of its beauty.

- Francis de Sales

The ultimate measure of a man is not where he stands in moments of comfort and convenience, but where he stands at times of challenge and controversy.

- Martin Luther King, Jr

Good works do not make a good man, but a good man does good works.

- Martin Luther

It is the function of perfection to make one know one's imperfection.

- St. Augustine of Hippo

†

Sir, my concern is not whether God is on our side; my greatest concern is to be on God's side, for God is always right.

- Abraham Lincoln

Human things must be known to be loved: but Divine things must be loved to be known.

- Blaise Pascal

A musician is not recommended for playing long, but for playing well; it is obeying God willingly, that is accepted; the Lord hates that which is forced, it is rather a tax than an offering. Cain served God grudgingly; he brought his sacrifice, not his heart.

- Thomas Watson

There is no such merchant as the charitable man; he gives trifles which he could not keep, to receive treasure which he cannot lose.

- Francis Quarles

†

Be not angry that you cannot make others as you wish them to be, since you cannot make yourself as you wish to be.

- Thomas a Kempis

How far that little candle throws his beams. So shines a good deed in a weary world.

- William Shakespeare

There is no more lovely, friendly or charming relationship, communion or company, that a good marriage.

- Martin Luther

By compassion we make others' misery our own, and so, by relieving them we relieve ourselves also.

- Thomas Browne, Sr.

†

Error of opinion may be tolerated where reason is left free to combat it.

- Thomas Jefferson

Depart from evil, and do good; seek peace, and pursue it.

- Psalm 34:14

The person who bears and suffers evils with meekness and silence, is the sum of a Christian man.

- John Wesley

There is no pillow so soft as a clear conscience.

- Unknown

Christianity is not a theory or speculation, but a life; not a philosophy of life, but a living presence.

- Samuel Taylor Coleridge

†

No one can make you feel inferior without your permission.

- Eleanor Roosevelt

Ye are the light of the world. A city that is set on an hill cannot be hid.

- Mathew 5:14

Seek the Lord and his strength; seek his presence continually!

- Psalm 105:4

A man should never be ashamed to own he has been in the wrong, which is but saying in other words that he is wiser today than he was yesterday.

- Alexander Pope

†

Jesus said unto him, If thou canst believe, all things are possible to him that believeth.

- Mark 9:23

For the grace of God that bringeth salvation hath appeared to all men, Teaching us that, denying ungodliness and worldly lusts, we should live soberly, righteously, and godly, in this present world...

- Titus 2:11-12

And then, what is grace? Grace is love. But grace is not love simply, and purely, and alone. Grace and love are, in their innermost essence, one and the same thing.

- Alexander Whyte

But Jesus beheld them, and said unto them, With men this is impossible; but with God all things are possible.

- Matthew 19:26

†

The happiness of the creature consists in rejoicing in God, by which also God is magnified and exalted.

- Jonathan Edwards

What a man says and what a man is must stand together.

- Maltbie Davenport Babcock

Kindness is the noblest weapon to conquer with.

- Thomas Fuller

A man may read the figures on the dial, but he cannot tell how the day goes unless the sun is shining on it; so we may read the Bible over, but we cannot learn to purpose till the spirit of God shine upon it and into out hearts.

- Thomas Watson

†

Faith consists in believing when it is beyond the power of reason to believe.

- Voltaire

The tests of life are to make, not break us. Trouble may demolish a man's business but build up his character. The blow at the outward man may be the greatest blessing to the inner man. If God, then, puts or permits anything hard in our lives, be sure that the real peril, the real trouble, is that we shall lose if we flinch or rebel.

- Maltbie Davenport Babcock

He who forgives ends the quarrel.

- Unknown

We should pray to the angels, for they are given to us as guardians.

- St. Ambrose

†

Prosperity is a great teacher; adversity is a greater. Possession pampers the mind; privation trains and strengthens it.

- William Hazlitt

Our lives are full of supposes. Suppose this should happen, or suppose that should happen; what could we do; how could we bear it? But, if we are living in the high tower of the dwelling place of God, all these supposes will drop out of our lives. We shall be quiet from the fear of evil, for no threatenings of evil can penetrate into the high tower of God.

- Hannah Whitall Smith

The generous who is always just, and the just who is always generous, may, unannounced, approach the throne of heaven.

- Johann Kaspar Lavater

†

If thou wouldst find much favor and peace with God and man, be very low in thine eyes; forgive thyself little and others much.

- Robert Leighton

God sends no one away empty except those who are full of themselves.

- Dwight Lyman Moody

Hope is like the sun, which, as we journey toward it, casts the shadow of our burden behind us.

- Samuel Smiles

Never think that God's delays are God's denials. Hold on! hold fast! hold out! Patience is genius.

- Georges L.L. de Buffon

†

Patience is the companion of wisdom.

- St. Augustine of Hippo

Men occasionally stumble over the truth, but most of them pick themselves up and hurry off as if nothing had happened.

- Winston Churchill

Make friends with the angels, who though invisible are always with you. Often invoke them, constantly praise them, and make good use of their help and assistance in all your temporal and spiritual affairs.

- Francis de Sales

Kind words do not cost much. Yet they accomplish much.

- Blaise Pascal

✝

Don't be overcome by evil, overcome evil with good.

- Romans 12:21

The soul, itself invisible, is seen by what it does through the body.

- Johann Albrecht Bengel

Love does not dominate; it cultivates.

- Johann Wolfgang Goethe

They, then, who are destined to die, need not be careful to inquire what death they are to die, but into what place death will usher them.

- St. Augustine of Hippo

†

What is a home without a Bible? 'Tis a home where daily bread for the body is provided, but the soul is never fed.

- Charles Meigs

One of the first things which a physician says to his patient is, 'Let me see your tongue.' A spiritual advisor might often do the same.

- Nehemiah Adams

Would you throw away a diamond because it pricked you? One good friend is not to be weighed against all the jewels of all the earth. If there is coolness or unkindness between us, let us come face to face and have it out. Quick, before the love grows cold. Life is too short to quarrel in, or carry dark thoughts of friends. It is easy to lose a friend, but a new one will not come for calling, nor make up for the old one when he comes.

- Leaves of Gold

†

There is a famine in America. Not a famine of food, but of love, of truth, of life.

- Mother Teresa

Great thoughts of your sin alone will drive you to despair; but great thoughts of Christ will pilot you into the haven of peace.

- Charles Haddon Spurgeon

Life would be a perpetual flea hunt if a man were obliged to run down all the innuendoes, inveracities, insinuations and misrepresentations which are uttered against him.

- Henry Ward Beecher

All who call on God in true faith, earnestly from the heart, will certainly be heard, and will receive what they have asked and desired.

- Martin Luther

†

Of all human activities, man's listening to God is the supreme act of his reasoning and will.

- Pope Paul VI

Ahab is born among us every day, and in this world he never ceases to exist.

- St. Ambrose

Impatient people water their miseries and hoe up their comforts; sorrows are visitors that come without invitation, and complaining minds send a wagon to bring their troubles home in.

- Charles Haddon Spurgeon

That which is striking and beautiful is not always good; but that which is good is always beautiful.

- Anne de l'Enclos

†

All that I am or ever hope to be, I owe to my angel Mother.

- Abraham Lincoln

All I have seen teaches me to trust the Creator for all I have not seen.

- Ralph Waldo Emerson

Art is a reflection of God's creativity, an evidence that we are made in the image of God.

- Francis Schaeffer

Never let us be guilty of sacrificing any portion of truth on the altar of peace.

- John Charles Ryle

†

For a small reward, a man will hurry away on a long journey; while for eternal life, many will hardly take a single step.

- Thomas a Kempis

No cloud can overshadow a true Christian but his faith will discern a rainbow in it.

- Bishop Horne

As God by creation made two of one, so again by marriage He made one of two.

- Thomas Adams

And the work of righteousness shall be peace; and the effect of righteousness, quietness and assurance for ever. And my people shall dwell in a peaceable habitation, and in sure dwellings, and in quiet resting places.

- Isaiah 32:17-18

†

I know why families were created with all their imperfections. They humanize you. They are made to make you forget yourself occasionally, so that the beautiful balance of life is not destroyed.

- Anais Nin

I have no greater joy than to hear that my children walk in truth.

- 3 John 1:4

Praise the LORD, O my soul, and forget not all his benefits-who forgives all your sins and heals all your diseases, who redeems your life from the pit and crowns you with love and compassion.

- Psalm 103:3-4

I've never been hurt by anything I didn't say.

- Calvin Coolidge

†

No flattery can heal a bad conscience, so no slander can hurt a good one.

- Thomas Watson

A characteristic of the flesh is its fickleness: it alternates between Yes and No and vice versa. But the will of God is: "Walk not according to the flesh (not even for a moment) but according to the Spirit.

- Watchman Nee

Christ is not valued at all unless He is valued above all.

- St. Augustine of Hippo

Sow a thought, reap an act; sow an act, reap a habit; sow a habit, reap a character; sow a character, reap a destiny.

- Unknown

†

Temptation is like a winter torrent, difficult to cross. Some, then, being most skillful swimmers, pass over, not being overwhelmed beneath temptations, nor swept down by them at all, while others who are not such, entering into them, sink in them. As, for example, Judas, entering into the temptation of covetness, swam not through it, but, sinking beneath it, was choked both in body and spirit. Peter entered into the temptation of the denial, but having entered it, he was not overwhelmed by it, but manfully swimming through it he was delivered.

- St. Cyril

Generosity always wins favor, particularly when accompanied by modesty.

- Johann Wolfgang Goethe

I would rather feel compassion than know the meaning of it.

- Thomas Aquinas

†

When it thunders, the thief becomes honest.

- Proverb

God does not give us everything we want, but He does fulfill His promises...leading us along the best and straightest paths to Himself.

- Dietrich Bonhoeffer

Many are ashamed to be seen as God made them; few are ashamed to be seen what the devil hath made them. Many are troubled at small defects in the outward man; few are troubled at the greatest deformities of the inward man...

- Abraham Wright

Longing desire prayeth always, though the tongue be silent. If thou art ever longing, thou art ever praying.

- St. Augustine of Hippo

†

Without the heart it is not worship; it is a stage play; an acting a part without being that person really a hypocrite. We may truly be said to worship God- though we lack perfection; but we cannot be said to worship Him if we lack sincerity.

- Stephen Charnock

Father! - to God himself we cannot give a holier name.

- William Wordsworth

Do you seek any further reward beyond that of having pleased God? In truth, you know not how great a good it is to please Him.

- John Chrysostom

The chains of habit are generally too small to be felt until they are too strong to be broken.

- Samuel Johnson

†

On earth we have nothing to do with success or its results, but only being true to God and for God; for it is sincerity and not success which is the sweet savor before God.

- Frederick W. Robertson

A truth that's told with bad intent beats all the lies you can invent.

- William Blake

✝

✝

May all creatures live in peace.

Printed in Great Britain
by Amazon.co.uk, Ltd.,
Marston Gate.